KU-424-860

What Do SCREWS Do?

Heinemann
LIBRARY

David Glover

 www.heinemann.co.uk/library
Visit our website to find out more information about Heinemann Library books.

To order:
☎ Phone 44 (0) 1865 888066
   Send a fax to 44 (0) 1865 314091
📄 Visit the Heinemann Bookshop at www.heinemann.co.uk/library to browse our
💻 catalogue and order online.

First published in Great Britain by Heinemann Library,
Halley Court, Jordan Hill, Oxford OX2 8EJ, part
of Harcourt Education. Heinemann is a registered
trademark of Harcourt Education Ltd.

Editorial: Clare Lewis and Katie Shepherd
Design: Victoria Bevan and Q2A Creative
Illustrations: Barry Atkinson (pp5, 15, 19), Douglas Hall
(p6) and Tony Kenyon (p4)
Picture Research: Mica Brancic
Production: Helen McCreath
Printed and bound in China by WKT Company
Limited

10 digit ISBN 0 431 06403 2
13 digit ISBN 978 0 431 06403 1
10 09 08 07 06
10 9 8 7 6 5 4 3 2 1

British Library Cataloguing in Publication Data
Glover, David
What do screws do? - 2nd Edition
621.8'82
A full catalogue record for this book is available from
the British Library.

Acknowledgements
The publishers would like to thank the following for
permission to reproduce photographs: Trevor Clifford
pp1, 4, 6, 7, 8, 9, 10, 11, 16, 18, 19; Robert Harding
Picture Library p12; Zefa pp13, 15; Spectrum Colo
Library p20.

Cover photograph reproduced with permission of Corb

The publishers would like to thank Angela Royston for
her assistance in the preparation of this book.

Every effort has been made to contact copyright
holders of any material reproduced in this book. Any
omissions will be rectified in subsequent printings if
notice is given to the publishers.

The paper used to print this book comes from
sustainable resources.

Any words appearing in the text in bold, **like this**, are
explained in the Glossary

Contents

What are screws?

A screw has a **groove** which winds round and round. The groove is a spiral shape. It is called a **thread**. When you turn a wood screw the thread cuts into the wood.

With each turn the screw is pulled into the wood by one thickness of the thread. After several turns the screw is firmly in place.

You could not push a screw into wood with your bare hands. The screw thread **magnifies** your strength by winding the screw in a little at a time.

With screw threads you can tighten and grip things. You can do this with much more force than you can by pushing or pulling.

FACT FILE Screw strength

Screws magnify your strength. All your effort to turn them is concentrated into small movements inwards.

one turn

spiral thread

forward movement

Lids and caps

This lemonade bottle has a screw cap. The top holds on tightly enough to stop the gas from escaping. You must remember to screw the cap back on tightly after you have poured a drink.

When you screw down the cap it squashes a small circle of card or plastic onto the neck of the bottle. This makes a tight **seal** that keeps in the gas.

Screw caps on jars help to keep food fresh. They seal tightly enough to stop **germs** getting into the jar. They also stop the food inside from drying out.

FACT FILE
Popping corks

Some fizzy drinks are stored in bottles with corks. The cork has to be held on with wire to stop it from popping out. These bottles are difficult to seal once they have been opened.

Nuts and bolts

Nuts and **bolts** hold things together. The **thread** on a bolt screws into the thread inside a nut.

You can use a **spanner** to tighten a nut. With a spanner you can make a nut so tight that it will hold the wheels on your bike. Nuts will even hold the engine in place inside a car.

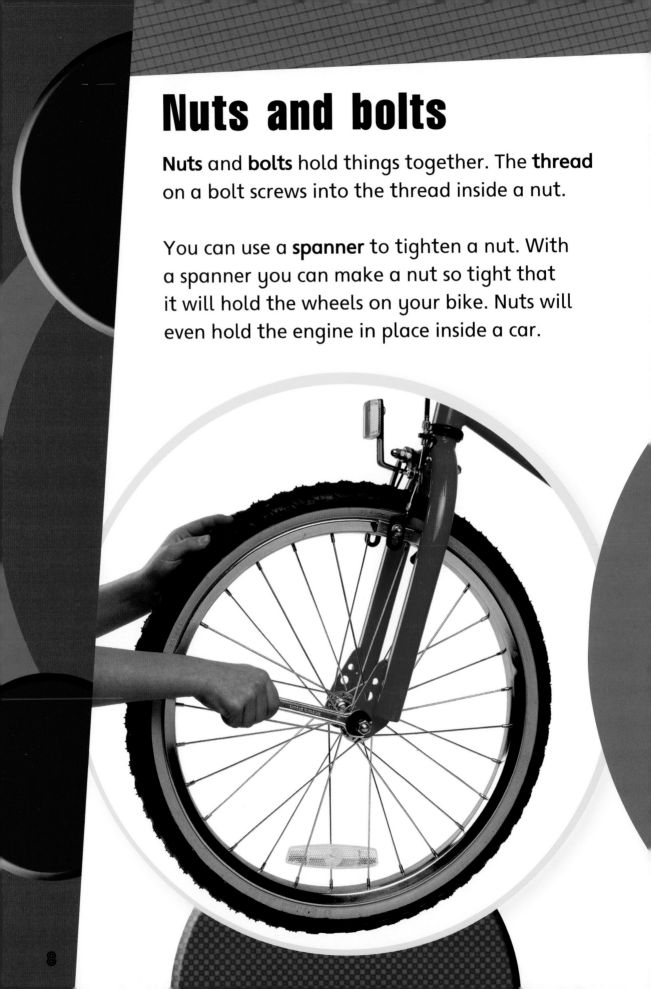

Nuts have different shapes. Some have wings so that you can turn them with your fingers. Some nuts are square. The most common shape is a hexagonal nut with six sides.

You can make a nut tighter with a spanner than you can with your fingers. A long spanner helps you tighten with more power than a short one.

Corkscrews and drills

As you turn a corkscrew it winds slowly into the cork. The corkscrew grips the cork tightly enough for you to pull the cork out of the bottle.

Sharp edges on the end of a drillbit cut into the wood. The drillbit has a spiral **thread**. The thread winds the waste wood back from the hole.

An **auger** is a very large drill. It is used to make big holes, for example to plant fence posts or trees. The auger has a wide screw thread. The thread winds the soil out of the hole.

drillbit

Staircases and slides

A spiral staircase is like a giant screw that you climb. You move up higher each time you go around the staircase. The spiral spreads the climbing over a longer distance. This means that each upward step takes less effort than when you climb straight up.

A spiral slide is great fun! Gravity (the force that makes things fall) pulls you down the slide. The spiral spins you around. A helter-skelter is a spiral fairground slide. Some water chutes use the same idea.

FACT FILE Which way round?

Spiral staircases nearly always go up clockwise. This means that as you go up you turn in the same direction as the hands on a clock. Most people find it easier to come down a spiral staircase when they move round anticlockwise.

Water screws

An Archimedes screw is a kind of **water pump**. It moves water from one place to another. The turning screw winds water up from a lower level to a higher one.

FACT FILE Ancient screws

Archimedes was a scientist in ancient Greece. He invented the Archimedes screw more than 2,000 years ago. It is a kind of pump that farmers in some countries still use today.

The **propeller** on this boat is a water screw. As the blades spin they push water backwards. This pushes the boat forwards in the same way as gas rushing backwards from a rocket or a jet engine.

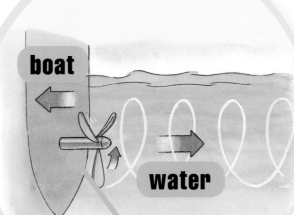

Hoses and taps

Lengths of garden hose are joined together with screw joints. The screw **threads** hold the pieces together tightly so that no water leaks out.

The water for the hose is turned on and off with a tap.

The screw inside the tap **magnifies** the force from your fingers as you turn the tap. The screw moves a rubber washer up or down. The washer blocks or unblocks a hole through which the water flows.

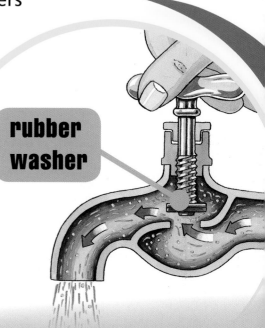

rubber washer

Squirting water

The force of the water inside a tap can be powerful. Turn on a garden hose and try to stop the water with your thumb. It squirts out everywhere!

Jacks and clamps

Can a small person lift a car with their bare hands? That person can using a **screw jack**. When the screw is turned, this **magnifies** the strength in the person's arms. The car rises a little at a time.

Warning: Screw jacks should only be used by adults. Lifting cars can be very dangerous.

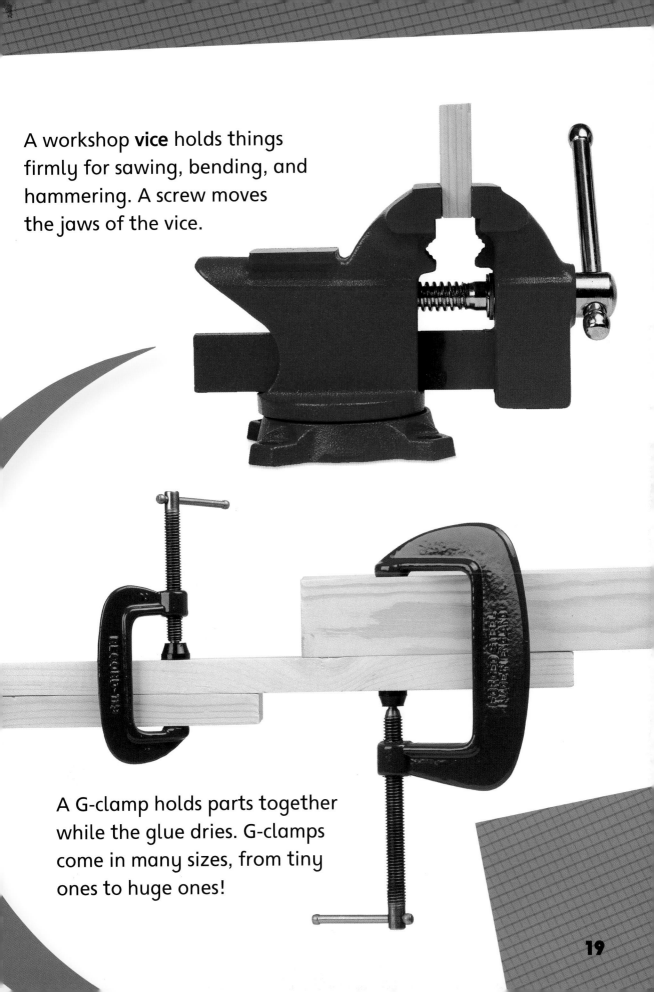

A workshop **vice** holds things firmly for sawing, bending, and hammering. A screw moves the jaws of the vice.

A G-clamp holds parts together while the glue dries. G-clamps come in many sizes, from tiny ones to huge ones!

Tunnel borers

How do you dig a tunnel under the sea-bed? You dig it with a machine that cuts through the rock like a giant drill.

Tunnel-boring machines are like giant drills. They have spinning **blades** at the front. As the machine is pushed forwards, the blades cut into the rock. The cut rock passes back through holes in the blades. It is taken out of the tunnel by train.

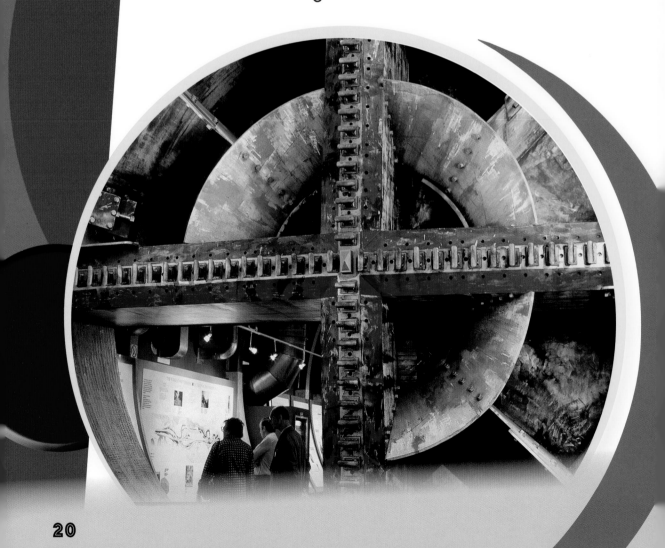

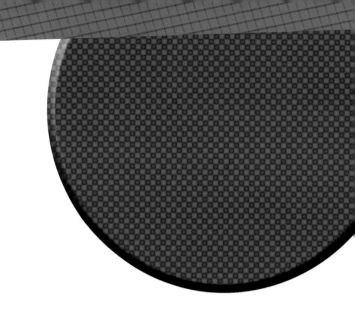

The Channel Tunnel goes under the sea between England and France. Eleven huge tunnel-boring machines took six years to build it.

FACT FILE **Perfect match!**

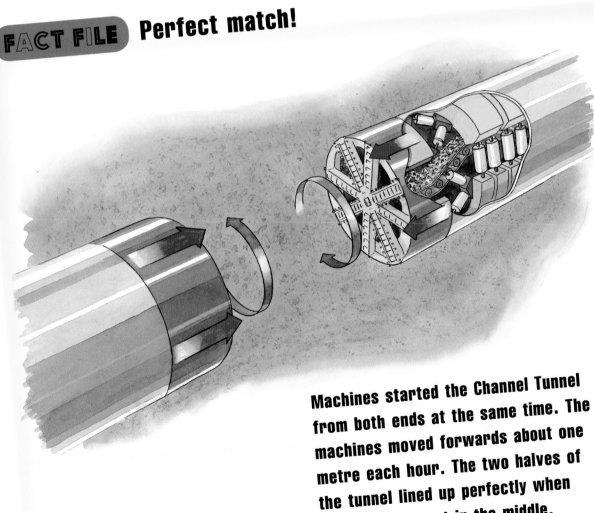

Machines started the Channel Tunnel from both ends at the same time. The machines moved forwards about one metre each hour. The two halves of the tunnel lined up perfectly when the machines met in the middle.

Activities

Screw it!

1. You need a piece of soft wood, a nail, some screws, and a screwdriver.
2. Use the nail to make a small hole in the wood.
3. Hold a screw steady in the hole.

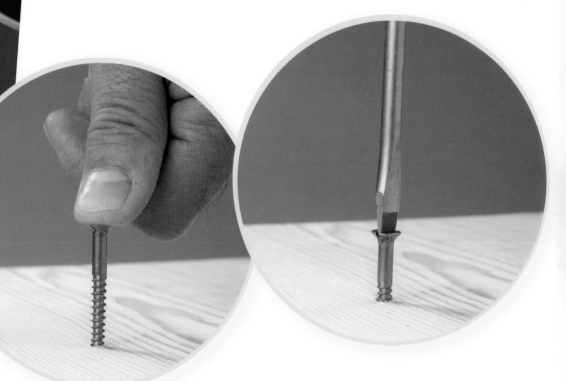

4. Can you push the screw into the wood using just your fingers?
5. Now use the screwdriver to push the screw into the wood.

See pages 4–5 to find out more about this.

Stop the flow!

1. You need a tap that turns to start or stop cold water flowing.
2. Turn on the tap.
3. Put your thumb or hand over the end of the tap to stop the water flowing. What happens?

4. Turn off the tap.
5. How does the tap stop the water flowing so easily?

See pages 16–17 for an explanation.

Glossary

auger   tool for drilling large holes

blade   the sharp cutting part of a knife

bolt   type of screw used with a nut, for holding things together

germs   micro-organisms which can cause disease

grooves   long narrow channels, cut into something

magnify   make bigger

nut   something which screws onto the end of a bolt to hold things together

propellers   blades which spin round to pull a plane through the air or push a boat through water

screw jack   machine used for raising heavy objects

seal   close something very tightly

spanner   tool used for turning a nut

thread   spiral groove around a bolt or screw

vice   instrument with jaws used for holding things steady

water pump   machine for raising water up from deep in the ground

Index